Think Yourself Young

Laugh Yourself to Life

Collected Poems of

Lea Hope Becker

Library of Congress Cataloging-in-Publication Data
Becker, Lea Hope
Think Yourself Young: Laugh Yourself to Life
p. cm.
Paperback ISBNs: 978-1-947708-02-0
Ebook ISBN: 978-1-947708-84-6
Library of Congress Control Number: 2020925333
First Edition, January 2021

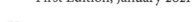 CITRINE PUBLISHING
(828) 585-7030
www.CitrinePublishing.com

To my very dear friend, Dorothy Glaze,
who passed away on November 18, 2019.
I credit our close friendship for
my being able to better access my
spiritual understanding of life.

Other Books By Lea Hope Becker

I Promise to Keep Quiet (After I'm Dead) *maybe

I Promise to Stay Married (This Time)

Children, I'm Home!

My Name's Not Robbie Any More

The Husband Who Kept His Wife Fat

Waking Up At Eighty-Three

When I first wake up in the morn
It feels worse than it felt to be born
Was I punished at night
For not sleeping just right?
Was my neck where my nightgown was worn?

When my feet first descend from the bedding
They're aware of the place where they're heading
But when they hit the floor
It's Nirvana no more
And there's hair on my pillow – I'm shedding!

Introduction

I'VE ALWAYS BEEN TRYING to make lemonade out of lemons and whimsy out of pathos, but I've never understood how I got this way. My earliest memory of finding methods for ending my toddler age crying jags was when I was about four years old. My Aunt May, ever filling in for my crazy clean mother who needed me out of the way as she polished our already polished furniture, told me something I've never forgotten:

"Cookie," she said (nobody in their right mind thought I matched the persona of my given name, Leah) "Life is very hard to get through, but you'll probably be okay."

"Why, Auntie?" I probably said, because questions rolled off my tongue like they were driven by gravity, "Why do you think I'll be okay?"

"Because, my child, you do have a sense of humor."

I didn't know what a sense of humor was, but if my aunt said I had it and that it was a good thing, I most likely figured out that it made sense to keep it from disappearing.

I've been pondering lately about how to maintain my cheerful nature, as my 83-year-old body is awash with minor ailments, like toenail fungus, arthritic joints here and there, failing hearing and a brain that has recorded every pop song of the '70s and keeps playing it back to me while I'm trying to sleep. Is this recollection the juice that's been generating my writing an abundance of material for so long?

As my life took many turns resulting in a dizzying number of residences in three different states, I amassed boxes of my creations and took them with me. They still hang out in my closet, under desks in my small office, in expandable wallet files on my bookshelves, and on countless thumb drives, floppy disks and a few CD's stored in hard to reach places.

I wrote my first actual rhyming verse at age ten and made the mistake of reading it to two of my girlfriends. They began laughing at me and followed it up with pre-adolescent abusive bullying that drove me to start a club for clubbish girls. After I had rounded up about six of us, we began to have meetings and I thought that I would have some relief from my totally dysfunctional family and a few neighbors that worried me. It didn't happen that way. I began writing silly rhymes and sometimes even sillier single sheet outpourings. Some of them sounded crabby, and others sounded hopeful. Today they call them essays.

In deciding to publish this assortment of rhyming slices of my life, I realized that since I'm a human, and humans have flaws, I needed to employ a character in my head that will signal me when I'm being a deviate. Just like the story in the movie, Pinocchio, there had to be a Jiminy Cricket, a conscientious kind of voice that would insert some sense into the flawed Pinocchio. Therefore, a conscience character will sometimes interfere with something I have included. Most of the time I will leave the material as is. I have named this character "Marlene." I'm the author, and I like that name.

P.S. I have arranged my included poems in categories, so that a person with a normal attention span (which is not normal for me) can choose what to dive into.

Contents

Health And Beauty?

The Pain Of Adapting To Change

Women's Tales Of Men

Youthful Memories
And Maternal Concerns

The Aging Author's Lament

Travel And Its After Effects

Modern Art

Quarantining Isn't Normal — Fretting Is

Optimism For The Pessimists

Antidote To Aging

Think Yourself Young

When your arthritis acts up
And your veins show up blue
And the calendar says
You've reached eighty-two

There's only one way
To stay in the game
You've got to trick nature
So your age stays the same

Just wear bright purple socks
And a Spiderman shirt
And walk like a soldier
Although your knees hurt

If you think it's all over
With the final bell rung,
The world looks much brighter
When you start to think young

Let your mind wander
Let your heart sing
Be good to yourself
Try to love everything

But to keep life worthwhile
Keep your Social Security
Maybe spend it on sex toys
Since there's no prize for purity.

Marlene & Me

Marlene: "So, just how is it possible to think yourself young? It's got to take more than just writing a few cute lines of verse!"

Me: "It does take quite a bit of work. The hardest part is how to avoid one's inclination to be mentally lazy, but . . ."

Marlene: "Not me! I work hard on my attitude every day! First I put on makeup and do my hair and that makes me feel good and ready to face the world. But by the time night comes, I'm a limp piece of linguini because the day has been so exhausting!"

Me: "Well, you can't dwell on such negative thoughts. They will make you weary and also make going to bed a real downer. When you wake up your brain will have gotten those messages and will start to agree with your feelings! Then the whole system starts to shut down!"

Marlene: "Like a computer? Shutting down? Then the screen goes blank!!"

Me: "Well, not exactly. The brain is the repository of all your lifetime learning – everything you've experienced to enhance your actions. Actually, that so-called gray matter in your head is an amazing encyclopedia — trouble is, it's just that as you get older it's harder to get to the right page!"

Marlene: "So is reviving my teen-aged dreams the answer?"

Me: "It depends on how you hold fast to those long ago dreams you had."

Marlene: "Sure, and I've now got this aging body. I'll never be 30 again!!!"

Me: "Who wants to be 30??? That was the age when we were still burping our babies!"

Marlene: Say, I thought I was supposed to be the Conscience! Oh, well, I will grant you this: Let's see what you're getting at. I'll try to have an open mind."

Older And Wiser?

My handicap tag allows me to park
Closer to stores, whether daylight or dark
I don't feel old until I start to walk
My voice is more gravelly whenever I talk

My brain's still quite active when I start to think
Our dishes get washed when I'm there at the sink
I fold all my laundry even neater than ever
But do I still jog? The answer is never

I drive my poor brain and I drive my small car
I'm not afraid to take it quite far
But there in my handbag, so heavily packed
Are meds and health needs and that is a fact

So how many years do I still think I've got?
To write just for fun and to laugh quite a lot?
It doesn't much matter if I think I should know
Just how many more days that I'm good to go!

Having The Right Bra

Marlene: "Why are you writing about something so personal? I wouldn't do it!"

Me: "What woman doesn't secretly think about what happens to you know what as you get older?"

Marlene: "I dunno, maybe women who have them altered?"

Me: Well, I'm letting mine be. But I'm willing to spend my heart out for the right, uh, container."

Marlene: "I guess you're the author. So do it."

* * *

It's not a big secret that as we gals age
We read lingerie ads on the skinny gal's page
Instead of the teeny, tiny boob picker-uppers
I've paid quite a price for too many rich suppers

The part that's supposed to be firm in one's youth
The part that once beckoned from the soda shoppe booth
Is now, if you'll permit me a crudity, a drag
The old strapless style in the drawer's now a rag

Don't some old women still want the American Dream?
My American Dream's a man still full of Steam
There are blouses to fill and sweaters to shape
And we all want that lovely full profile to drape

So forget the ten-cent store, it's lost in the past
Avoid the undies sale, where teen types are massed
Pass up those Asian-made things made of cotton
To me, a size 34-A's long forgotten

If I want to look hot with some fine restoration
If I want a great line while I'm on vacation
I head straight to Neiman's — the home of the brave
Where money means nothing and there's no need
to save

Where the lingerie area has carpet so thick
And the velvet-voiced saleslady approaches so quick
She's dying to help me buy linens and laces
She's accustomed to ostrich bags and Givenchy faces

I pick out my favorite — with embroidery and wire
And then another color which I'm prone to admire
I clasp it behind me myself, if I'm able
I check out the price and the very French label

If I hold my breath at the price tag, my friend
My bra will fit better – will my wallet extend?
With my purchases wrapped in fine tissue and bagged
I gaze at the peignoirs electronically tagged

But my budget's limited and so is my time
And I tell myself "Dearie, you're not in your prime!"
If I had my way, I'd have more than one closet
When my checkbook cried "stop," I'd make one big
deposit

At home while I model my shapely old bod
My husband comes in and exclaims, "Oh My God!"
(He noticed the Neiman's bag crammed in the trash
And noticed the lesser amount in our stash)

"But Honey," I stammer, "Honey, how do I look?"
His eyes not on me, he says "Is tonight when you cook?"
So wearing my elegant bra from South France,
I trudge to the kitchen, wearing old knee-worn pants.

I Love South Florida Weather

Marlene: "This is another story poem with the same meter as the one about the boobs. Why are you following with. . . ."

Me: "This one's also about a woman's body and how she wants to feel."

Marlene: "Well, at least it's upbeat. Go for it!"

I love South Florida weather — I do!
If humidity's good for you, you'll love it too
Early morning I'm outside and checking the weather
And I soon feel my boobs kind of sticking together

Sometimes I go to our community pool,
I'd swim in the ocean, but I'm not a fool
I'd rather watch surfers with no inhibitions
I'm scared of big waves plus some other conditions

Our pool's one that's heated, but my legs still look blue
Maybe that's why other swimmers are few
Sometimes the pool's heating system breaks down
Is that when those poolside folks flee right to town?

I asked my friend next door who often feels glum
"Go with me swimming, Mae, you're such a good chum!"
Mae looked at me like I'd just said something wrong
"You think I'm some model who wears a sarong?"

My lesson was learned – some women won't wear
A bathing suit anywhere or mess up her hair
So I go alone with my poolside supplies
Prepared to start sweating while swatting the flies

No sooner do I slap that sun block in place
Remove my sunglasses while tanning my face
When suddenly an ominous sound can be heard
It isn't an airplane or an awfully big bird

It's thunder still distant, a gathering storm
Then the wind starts to blow and I'm no longer warm
I would warn other sunbathers, but no one is there
I'm the one dumb bunny decked out on a chair

And while I start running and making new plans
I still worship the beach and the pool and the tans
I'm one of the flock, like birds of a feather
I told you, I'm crazy about Florida weather!

Limping With Flair

Marlene: "I peeked! This one's a limerick! You must have cracked a book about the origin of this type of poetry!"

Me: "I have a book like that, actually. It's all about how poetry has undergone changes."

Marlene: "Did you actually read it?"

Me: "Never got past the table of contents. I wrote my first limerick after I traveled to Dublin with my husband and asked a pub crawler for directions to our hotel after we got lost."

Marlene: "I don't get the connection."

Me: "That's the point. Truth is, I have no idea how I came up with this meter — only when."

* * *

I had a knee surgeon who thrived
On patients whose strides were deprived
Their walking was stilted
They often walked tilted
And needed help as they survived

Once I became one of those ailing
My morning jaunts seemed to be failing
So I came to this doc
(And would go into hock)
Just to live my next years with smooth sailing

The doc checked me out with precision
Before making his medical decision
"I can fix up your knee,
But you'll have to agree:
Exercise is your newest religion!"

So I got on the treadmill and bike
Took more stairs (which I never did like)
Every morning I rose
Bravely donning my clothes
Or my new knee would soon go on strike!

Though my mindset was sometimes to coddle
Like my one-year-old learning to toddle
My new standard of care
Was to walk with a flair
And pretend I'm a *Vogue* fashion model!

Put The Sweater On — Take The Sweater Off

My thermostat's confused
That's why I'm such a mess
Sometimes I'm up, then down
Sometimes I have to guess

I take my sweater off
But feel cold fairly fast
I put my sweater on
My comfort doesn't last

On any given day
No matter, warm or cold
I might feel either way
It happens when you're Old

I move that thermostat
The fan was off, now on
No matter where I'm at
Or what I'm perched upon

More comfort is compelling
As elderly status looms
I need a special dwelling
With differently heated rooms

I'm tired of complaining
I've got to get a grip
It's better to get older
Than body temperature zip

My Falling Face

My poor face is falling
It is, yes indeed
My eyelids no longer
Can get up to speed

I'm thinking quite young
While feeling quite crappy
It's tough to be carefree,
And hard to stay happy!

I try to walk briskly
At my own glacial pace
While my decades are walking
All over my face

My muscles feel wooden
My knee joints do too
They all need some fixing
But where is the glue?

Why does life get stressful
With fears and concerns?
There's lots to feel good about
Good fortune takes turns

So back to my mirror now
I'll release a small sigh
My engine's still running
While my face starts to die!

Oil Change

The car needed quick lubrication
Why burn out a good working part?
We serviced it while on vacation
Keeping the car oiled is smart

While idling inside the waiting room
I thought about all my poor joints
They needed servicing just like my car
I pondered these worrisome points

The vehicle always comes in first
When deciding what to repair
But my bones and muscles must wait in line
Don't I deserve customized care?

My back aches whenever I'm lifting
My knee creaks whenever I walk
My feet hurt when standing is lengthy
My brain stalls sometimes when I talk
Folks pray to achieve health and wisdom
In a welcoming church with a steeple
So why not tell God we have one more request
A Jiffy Lube just for us people.

Trying To Learn Spanish
(When You're Already Forgetting
Some English Words)

I've wanted to be bi-lingual
For a seriously long long time
I've tried to learn some Spanish
But my pronunciation's a crime;

In order to learn a language
You need to try conversing
With everyday Spanish people
Think of it as rehearsing;

But here's the big *problema*
My memory's not so *caliente*
No sooner do I *aprendo lo*
When I get lost in the verbal *fuente*

I've thought of ways around it
Like tape deck lessons while driving
Then while reaching my destination,
I'd get *mas intelligente* while arriving;

But knowing my usual pitfalls
I fear the following scenario
I get to the place where I'm going
And my mind goes blank in the barrio;

The Spanish word for panic
Is *panico*, so I'm told
And if confidence is *confianza*,
Am I too *tarde* or too old?

They say if you really want to
You can learn anything *nuevo* with ease
But it's not so *facil* to learn something
When your *cabeza* gets in a deep freeze;

I believe I really *intento*
But my brain makes other plans
The new Spanish goes in some closet
While I wring my linguistic hands;

They say if you hang out with Latins
Your fluency magically grows
So why do my Spanish friends laugh out loud
Hearing my broken Spanish prose?

I don't mind entertaining them
I'd even do a little dance
Maria, please don't think me *absurdo*
José, please give me another chance!

Health And Beauty?

The Doctor's Waiting Room

Whenever I visit the doctor
I'm so ill at ease but I'm curious
Are the waiting room patients not healthy?
Or do they have complaints somewhat spurious?

The receptionists are always too busy
You put your name down on their list
The foot traffic makes you quite dizzy
If you left, would you even be missed?

You're reading health journals forever
Or you may have arrived somewhat late;
They'll call out your last name whenever,
Oops! sometimes you had the wrong date;

You've either been good or quite naughty
It really does not matter which
You hope that the medics aren't haughty
Regarding your pain, cold or itch;

You know your chart's in a collection
That includes the sick and the dying
You come there for your health protection
But the fact is, you're prone to be lying;

You're there since you know your attendance
Is the easiest thing you can do
You're a sinner and this is repentance
But absolution is just for the few;

No matter how often you come there
The ordeal doesn't get any sweeter
You continue to feel very dumb there
They all know you're a visit repeater!

So with all of my fool's trepidation,
I guess I can handle the stress
I might even feel some elation —
I've still got some years, more or less!

Nutrition Ambition

I ask my good doctor
"Oh what shall I eat?
I need to lose weight but still
Stay on my feet!"
He hands me a list
Recommending the stuff
That my body needs
Or it won't get enough

I read through the list
It had two different sections
One was food items
The other directions
There's so many veggies
But nix on red meat
Does he have concern
On my best thing to eat?
"Say, doc, on this list here,
You vetoed my steak
But clearly you voted

For occasional cake. . .
I've already quit pastry
And cookies and sweets
So I'm a bit miffed
That you don't like red meats!
"I'm a carnivore, sir
I've always been such
If I can't eat that meat
I won't like it much
I'll wolf down that spinach
And broccoli too
But pass up filet?
What's wrong with a zoo?"

The doctor stands up
And has an expression
That seeks to discourage
My eating aggression
"You asked for a diet —
I performed that task
If you didn't want it
Then why did you ask?"

"I guess I'm conflicted
I want to be thin
But if it's not magic
Then don't count me in!
If veggies and lo-cal
Is all that I need
Then I'll try to do it
For one week, indeed!

But if I'm unhappy
And don't lose that much
I'll go back to red meat
I know it's a crutch"
So I returned home
With my new resolution
Bought spinach and kale
For my diet solution

And after I'd lost
About seventeen pounds
I went back to steak
(I know how that sounds)

When folks are carnivorous
Like I've always been
They hate to change habits
Even though they're not thin

Today in the newspaper
What news did I see?
Twas a column on red meat
New researchers see
That red meat's not bad
It isn't a clogger
Of everyone's arteries
Well I'll be a blogger!

I'm going to news feed
And let the docs know
That I've ignored their diets
And I'm still good to go!
But now that I'm older
So smart, yeah, you guessed it
My rib-eye steak's waiting
For me to digest it!

Marlene: "Wait just a minute, now, so your favorite is rib-eye steak? And it has so much fat. What about all those calories?"

Me: "Well, there's still some controversy about whether carbs are worse!"

Marlene: "So you think you can get away with your obstinacy about only eating what you like?"

Me: "Well, Mr. Hershey ate a pound of chocolate every day and lived to be one hundred!"

Marlene: "And some people smoke all their lives and live long and prosper!"

Me: "Are you some Vulcan or something?"

Marlene: "I can't answer. Right now I'm not in a very good mood."

Me: "Try to stay cheerful."

Marlene: "I will, but you shouldn't have told me about Mr. Hershey. I'm dying for a chocolate-covered strawberry. That usually perks me up!"

Me: Some conscience! Can't you just tough it out?"

Marlene: "When did you become such a smartass?"

The Happy Old Lady Patient

The doctors all love me — I'm just eighty-two
I see ten specialists — how many do you?
My pharmacist gloats when I finally appear
She knows that her job will be safer this year

I had my knee fixed and walk a bit funny
My pills of all colors might be worth all the money
The two-sided mirror right next to my sink
Reminds me that I'm someone poised on the brink

If I have a new pain, I wonder, "where is it?"
And which medic now gets my follow-up visit
There's little uncertainty I'm not getting younger
But for life and good food, I've not lost my hunger

It's tough to be me, but delightful to breathe
I watched my first baby cry out and then teethe
My school days were trying but when I got out
It took me some time to learn what life's about

So now that I'm wiser and wrinkled and shorter
And frail like an old store of clay bricks and mortar
I'm writing my memoirs and reviewing my Will
And laughing my sides out while I climb that hill.

Toenails

I don't drink, I'm just not a boozer
But some body parts will decline
My feet seem to be my big loser
With my toenails at the front of the line

I've painted those nails with red polish
To cover the fact that they're weak
I'd like to wear low heels or flip-flops
But that possibility seems bleak

I've wrestled with aging foot fungus
And tried different highly priced creams
I go to the foot doctor quarterly
As he works I've suppressed many screams

But when he is through his assistant
Comes in with her high-powered file
She does a great job while I fantasize
That I'll soon wear new thongs that have style

"Will I keep my toenails forever?"
I hesitantly ask the young trimmer
She lowers her eyes and says, "Maybe,"
Is retaining those nails getting dimmer?

The answer, I fear, is not easy
My toenails might not last as long
As stuff that I store in my closet
Should I write a toenail swan song?

My Left Knee Isn't Right!

My left knee isn't right
My right knee feels left out
I'm walking rather tilted
Don't know what it's about!

My hearing's somewhat cockeyed
Would you repeat that last?
My right ear heard you better
They both don't work so fast!

When I look at my eyebrows
They don't seem to align
I wonder "What's the problem?"
Is this a troubling sign?

I know I'm getting older
But was it overnight?
My symmetry's disappearing
My left's not like my right!

Serenity Prayer For Foodaholics

I cannot change my DNA
It came from Mom and Daddy
My shape devolved from strands that way
Like every lass and laddie

But what I see and how I act
Is based on thoughts unique
As human, how will I react
And what goals will I seek?

My wisdom comes from endless search
My actions come through quest
Decisions not from temple or church
What food shall I ingest?

Belly Up To The Scale

I found myself watching my neighbor next door
When she glanced right at me, I looked down at the floor
I knew she was eighty plus years, maybe more
But she seemed oh so trim in the outfit she wore
"She's got great genes," I would grumble and wale
"That lady next door is as thin as a rail!"
But next to her appetite, mine would so pale
I said to myself: "Belly up to the scale."

I get really vexed at a weighing machine
It judges me no matter which way I lean
Sometimes I kick it when I feel quite mean
Whoever invented the dieting scene?

I wasn't born given a glamorous shape
Did they pinch me too hard in my poor little nape?
They all called me "chubby" — I couldn't escape
While I ate lunch at school, my friends would all gape

As my teen years flew by, my weight settled down
I starved myself, winning a weight-losing crown
To cover my misery, I hammed like a clown
No words could describe me, not one verb or noun

How many, you ladies, have told this same tale?
We all want our beauty and don't want to fail
We'd probably gain even landing in jail —
Imprisoned, some chocolates would come in the mail!

My friends think I'm witty — I make them all laugh
I write books which get signed with my cute autograph
At my last signing bash gained a pound and a half
I cringe at young teenagers, each a giraffe

As this decade passes, I really do wonder
What hell I've been in and which spell I've been under
I've craved slimming outfits but plans went asunder
If I do one more fad diet I'll be rotunder!

So I pass up the croissants and all rich desserts
I've been able and stable and buy smaller skirts
My husband has praised me "You're lovely!" he blurts
But I still kick that miserable scale 'til it hurts.

How To Toast A Bagel

I don't really fancy my food colored brown
When a bagel's like that, I just can't get it down
So I have a routine which works every time
I must set the toaster to stop on a dime.

First I slice the whole bagel so each half is thin
Each toastable half an identical twin
If I smell a hint of charcoal or worse
I throw the thing out in the garbage pail hearse

I know I've been told that the poor and ill-fed
Would gladly wolf down my rejected brown bread
I must be a mad woman crazy with shtick
But the thought of dark bagels still makes me feel sick

So I must pop my bagel just as it turns gold
And paste it with jam so I don't catch a cold
One day when I'm older and getting mature
I'll switch out of bread and eat celery, I'm sure

Oh Mama, you raised me an eating misfit!
When you pried my mouth open at first, did I spit?
If there were no bagels would my clothes still feel tight?
Or would I be thinner, with less cellulite?

The Pain Of Adapting To Change

I Wonder Who's Pushing Me Now

I miss the old songs that were sung
When I was still naïve and young
I feared the new dances
And wouldn't take chances
Being out of the loop surely stung

But growing up started to change me
New habits did soon rearrange me
I penned gripes to write
And then entered the fight
The mirror in my room showed a strange me!

I needed to modernize quickly
Despite some new ways that felt tickly
Each new step had a catch
Like an itch you can't scratch
Being stubborn is senseless and prickly!

Don't Drive Under The Influence Of Aggravation

Marlene: "Sometimes I have to drive. And I'm usually aggravated."

Me: "You should know me by now. I have to exaggerate sometimes. Why are there so many car accidents? Does anybody ever take a survey about the underlying causes?"

Marlene: "There are surveys about everything these days."

Me: "Well, I think folks should be more careful."

Marlene: "I agree."

Me: "Good, you can keep your job."

Marlene: "What job? You're not paying me zip!"

* * *

Don't drive when you're sleepy
Don't drive when you're creepy
Don't drive when you're dumb
Don't drive when you're numb

Don't drive when you're irritated
Don't drive when you're aggravated
Don't drive when it's slick
Don't drive when you're sick

Don't drive when you're dizzy
Don't drive when you're busy
Don't drive when you're faint
Don't drive when you caint

Don't drive when you're robotic
Don't drive when you're neurotic
Don't drive when you're testy
Don't drive when you're pesty

What I'm now thinking of
Is if I'm any of the above
I should leave home my car
Even if I have to go far

I can walk to the store
I can walk more and more
But I know if it's hot
That I can't walk a lot

I can walk to work out
I can walk when I pout
I can walk with poor vision
I can walk with derision

I can walk with emotion
I can walk with devotion
I can walk feeling sadness
I can walk having gladness

I can't drive with frustration
Or intense aggravation
I can't drive with dementia
With my brain in absentia

And since I'm now older
With an ache in each shoulder
I should probably chill out
That's what today is about

So in final conclusion
Safe driving's an illusion
When you get behind the wheel
No matter how you feel

You're taking a chance
You'll never again dance
But I'm staying on the highway
For I must do it MY WAY!

Why I Don't Play Golf

Marlene: "Say, in that poem about driving, why did I think I was reading Dr. Seuss? Now, on this Golf thing, who gives a hoot about what you do for entertainment or to stay active?"

Me: "All my friends who play golf."

Marlene: "Aren't you being a bit of a, uh, a coward?"

Me: "Read the poem. It will answer your questions."

* * *

I don't play golf for a number of reasons
I don't like to stand in the sun (or the shade)
I don't like to walk in the much warmer seasons
I don't think I'd like it if good golfers played

I don't think my ego could stand looking silly
I don't like the idea of swinging a club
I don't like terrain that is flat or quite hilly
I don't like to look for a ball in a shrub

I don't want to look like a golfing beginner
I don't want to spend on a sport that costs dough
I don't want new golf shorts if I can't be thinner
I don't want to learn if I can't be a pro

I don't want to work like an athlete in training
I don't want to feel muscle cramps anywhere
I don't want to be on the course when it's raining
I don't want to be on the course when it's fair

I don't want to be a poor sport for not trying
I don't want golf teachers to coach me at all
I don't want to land in a sand trap while crying
I don't want exertion if the grass is too tall

I don't want to make up excuses for losing
I don't want to try having confidence now
I don't want to do something not of my choosing
I don't want to try if I'll never learn how

So now I've been truthful about my ambition
I'll go to my grave never risking a drive
I'll never be steeped in retirement tradition
I'll just be an expert at staying alive.

Volunteering

Marlene: "I didn't know you spent any time volunteering. You like money too much."

Me: "It's called 'networking.' I had to do something when I moved to Florida and didn't know anybody. I thought I'd meet people and enjoy helping out."

Marlene: "So did you like doing it?"

Me: "I loved it. But would I have done it if I had foreseen how much work there was? I'm not sure. But I did meet a lot of people and it was fun."

Marlene: "So you're not just wanting to line your wallet?"

Me: I've always dreamed about becoming affluent."

Marlene: "And now?"

Me: "Can't a woman change her attitude?"

Marlene: "No comment."

* * *

Volunteering is like paying rent
You put out and you don't get a cent
At the end of the day
You don't count up your pay
You just total up how well you meant

You meet lots of folks who are pleasant
You talk to those chaps who are present
They're all just like you
Putting out at the zoo
It's a new way to feel like a peasant

The organization you serve
Is worthy, they surely deserve
Your finest attention
And I need to mention
They don't let you off the preserve

If you really need a vacation
From shlepping or lack of elation
You stay home, all right
But they call you that night
They just couldn't stand separation

For them you will go to the wall
You forget that you're really on call
You're a good human being
With your slave mates agreeing
A true volunteer has it all

Just think of the taxes you're saving
With no compensation while slaving
You knew when you started
You'd not be half-hearted
Was it brownie points that you were craving?

Don't think of yourself as a flunky
Just because you're a non-profit junkie
Now you have no more time
And they can't spare a dime
And your old geezer crowd thinks you're spunky!

If your bottom line says you're "retired"
And you gloat that you cannot be fired
Have another think, chum
Don't be naive or dumb
Get a clue how your brain cells are wired

If we try discontinuing our service,
In a day or two we would be nervous
With no work actuality
We would soon face reality
And think, "Did they really deserve us?"

If all volunteers went on strike
I wonder what life would be like
Would things still feel so sweet,
With no deadline to meet?
Would employment rolls suddenly spike?

So I'm ready to go to the "boss"
I sure hope that she doesn't get cross
If I no longer show up
Will everything blow up?
When I'm gone, would they soon feel the loss?

So now that I'm home needing pity
Being bored with the day's nitty-gritty
My withdrawal pains flicker
While I'm getting sicker
Guess I'll go back to Volunteer City

My Self-Driving Car

Marlene: "You won't live long enough to drive one of those things!"

Me: "You don't know that. Maybe I'll do it just for the publicity!"

Marlene: "Be my guest. Kill yourself."

Me: "They'll figure out how to make them safe, but it will be when your grandchildren become of driving age."

Marlene: Go ahead — publish this poem. I never thought I'd live to see marijuana legalized."

* * *

I bought me a self-driving car
Named "Christine," she could cruise fairly far
I'd just sit in the back
Nibbling nuts from my pack
Counting how many Starbucks there are

The car would respond to my call
"Hey, Christine, please pull into that mall.
There's a Starbucks right there
Park right here, I don't care,
And please order a bold coffee, tall."

I'd then slurp down my brew with delight
Thinking, "I'm really doing all right!"
"I can just take a nap,
"Get some rest — it's a snap!
"I could probably watch sitcoms tonight!"

So Christine knew that she had the con
I had told her what route we were on
But with voice recognition
There's one key condition
T'was the interface we were upon

If I spoke slightly slow she would hear it
But sometimes she was off and would queer it
So I tried to talk fast
Getting through her at last
So she'd reach the right place (at least near it!)

In our neighborhood we had no trouble
She could whisk me to Target on the double
But the car had her pride
If to places far and wide
The car's system would gurgle and bubble

Did I need to have this type of worry?
I'm a busy gal needing to hurry
So I boned up on tech
Didn't need a car wreck
Read the manual until I saw blurry!

Well, the manual said I should cool it
Just pamper the car when I fuel it
Give perfect directions
She had passed all inspections
So I practiced in a way not to fool it

"Now, Christine, out of state's where we're heading,
I'm due at my first cousin's wedding!"
Well, we never got there
The damned car didn't care
There's this older car I'll soon be getting!

* * *

Marlene: "Who's Christine? Why that name? Oh, yeah, that Steven King movie about a car!"

People Who Use Computers

People . . . People at computers
Are the grumpiest people
I have seen
Computers
Computers who need people
Do not fear an occasional fit
Although someone's throat is slit

Cause it's just someone grumpy
Being jumpy

Windows . . .
Mr. Gates' darling Windows
Is the loveliest OS
In the land

And when it crashes
Turns your stuff to ashes
You'll be consoled with a yellow warning
And it won't wake up in the morning
Cause it's just computers
Dissing people.

Yesterday I Accomplished ...Nothing!

After the tumult of another tax season
I wanted to rest without needing a reason
I desired to sit on my butt the whole day
If idleness was in, I would go all the way

So I carefully avoided projects and tasks
I thought to myself: (I hope no one asks)
For help with some problem or certain advice
Just to take a day off would be so very nice

I ate my three meals, but did not ride my bike
TV was okay and I watched what I like
My Things To Do list could be gathering dust
For one lousy day off, would I really go bust?

The phone on my desk could be ringing or not
The message machine could fill up on the spot
No power on earth could get me off the couch
I'd recline and veg out and walk tall with a slouch

The hours could crawl and the pace could be slow
Even driving was out — there was no place to go
I picked up a book and began Chapter One
Then I put the book down, since my reading was done

By evening my boredom was growing intensely
Could I be a gal who loved working immensely?
Or was it the change in routine that was tough?
I really can't answer, but I'd had enough

To really relax like a pro takes some guts
I'd have to observe those who sit on their butts
I'd have to learn patience and yoga and quiet
It's not so impossible — at least I could try it

But when I examine my motives, I fear
It's change that intimidates — that much is clear
I must be a routine-a-holic, that's me
So at sun-up tomorrow I'll busily be!

Yesterday's Gone — Should You Save Your Old Tinkertoys?

Marlene: "Did you really save your Tinker toys?"

Me: "No, I was worse. I saved my old poems, even the ones I began writing at age 10."

Marlene: "So why did you entitle this poem with the mention of "Tinker toys?"

Me: "I've been to antique malls, and outdoor flea markets. There's always somebody who's selling something that kids played with when I was a kid. It might as well be 'Tinker toys.' Besides, it sounds more lyrical than to use the brand name: 'Lincoln Logs.' "

Marlene: "Were your childhood writings any good?"

Me: "They were okay for my age level."

Marlene: "Why don't you put one of the best of them in this book?"

Me: "Maybe, after I die."

Since yesterday's toys are a thing of the past
And you're going to clean out your storage at last
Old memories hit you when you were a child
If your ball hit a window, you thought you were wild

Remember your bike with only one speed
You didn't have clothing that you didn't need
Your telephone number was four digits long
"By The Old Mill Stream" was your favorite song;

You remember no Santa Claus — how your dear mother lied
You remember how you felt when FDR died
When war was a good thing and protesting was not
When you slept on the floor when the summer was hot

You didn't have backpacks when you went to school
The smartest of pupils showed off his slide rule
Few girls tried out for track or ice hockey
But they each had a crush on the local disk jockey

The term "diversity" was a spelling bee word
And you thought that a "geek" was some kind of bird
You didn't sue the school if a teacher offended
You pigged out on sodas when the school year
was ended

But aside from your memories, getting back to your toys
When girls whispered at parties and boys would be boys
You didn't have video games at which to spend hours
Is that why you still love your Tinker Toy towers?

If you stroll down the aisles of today's Big Box store
You think kids of today would find old toys a bore
Would E-Bay perusers want to pay for your stuff?
If your toys had been used, they would not pay enough

So get with the program and throw out your past
You'll have room in your closets for your gym gear at last
What? Throw out old records with musical bliss?
Your search engine's there if you must reminisce.

I'll Never Become A Virgin Again

Me: Marlene, you're so quiet? Why aren't you commenting on this choice of titles?"

Marlene: "I'm afraid if I laugh, I'll choke."

Me: "So, is that a compliment?"

Marlene: "Aargghhh!"

* * *

I'll never become a virgin again
But I still have thoughts of "Remember When"
My bike saddle was my biggest elation
I dreamed of love on my family's vacation

My innocence was so pure and naive
I'd live in a garden and dance and believe
But even flowers have to bear seeds
The World is full of such mischievous deeds

My mother knew well the truth about kids
She disposed of my comic books plus high school bids
I guess she prepared me for marital life
My future was sealed with the cake with the knife

So as part of this Planet I end this refrain
I'll never become a virgin again!!!

Women's Tales
Of Men

At Big Mike's Cabana Bar

Marlene: "Is there such a place?"

Me: "Well, if there isn't, there should be."

Marlene: "Is this poem based on a true story?"

Me: "Well, if I wrote about it, then it must have happened to me during my dating years."

Marlene: "Like when you were between husbands?"

Me: "No comment."

* * *

Sitting at Big Mike's Cabana Bar
Before my Tequila shake
When will the geezer next to me
Begin to put on the make?

Rehearsing what I will say to him
Is it "I'm not that kind of girl?"
He turns to face me with his good eye
His gray moustache starting to curl

"Oh Ma'am, can I ask you a question?
You seem like a nice friendly sort;
Some women just won't speak to strangers —
Why one almost took me to court!"

I looked at the guy with a tremble
Wondering where this would go
Was he going to ask for my number?
(At least all his moves had been slow!)

I smiled as I made my decision
"My name is: Ilona La Combe!
I'm here to watch waves on this ocean."
Would I soon be inside his home?

He moved his left arm, which was hairy
And brought it right up to his ear
My heartbeat began to pump faster
Was there actually something to fear?
"I'm weary," he said while I waited
"Those beach stairs were too big a climb!
So if I might now ask you, Madam,
Could you please just tell me the time?"

Computer Dating For The Over-55 Woman

When new technology first came to my house
With me being single and seeking a spouse
I tried out a company promising men
Who would contact me soon and what would come then?

I submitted some photos, I'd put on some weight
But I really desired a prince for a date
One man who had seen me and thought I was cute
Called me up very shortly, seemed nice, not a brute!

He told me he'd worked a small farm, since retired
Loved animals and plants and for me was all fired
The man asked if casual dress was okay
I answered, "No problem, I like it that way!"

We met at a restaurant outside the door
And began with a handshake, too soon to have more!
The hostess directed us right to a table
He seemed quite well built and physically able

However, the first conversation was stilted
He gazed at the tablecloth, eyes downward tilted
His casual dress was designed to look poor
His blue jeans were ragged and smelled of manure

I'd gone to the beauty salon, hair and nails done
The outfit I'd chosen was my number one
The phone conversation had seemed so delightful
But meeting the guy turned out dreadful and frightful

I'm not against farming or casual dress
And shyness is not such a problem, I guess
But wasn't I worth wearing freshly washed jeans?
We weren't two youngsters still naïve in our teens

He phoned me again, on the next business day
For a second date with him? My thought was "No way!"
"Is there anything wrong, won't you give us a try?"
Now what could I answer this casually dressed guy?

I told him I'd enjoyed our restaurant date
But to see him again, it was really too late
I'd gotten involved with an old friend I knew
And was getting engaged soon, though it wasn't true

I've never been brave and was in quite a quandary
On how to advise a man he should do laundry
Or that simple eye contact would have been really nice
That dating technology should have come with advice!

* * *

Marlene: "This has to be a true story – you couldn't make it up!"

Me: "I exaggerated a little – the brown spots on his blue jeans must have been manure from his farm, but I'm not certain I could smell the jeans. It wouldn't have been appropriate to get that close to his pants on a first date."

Marlene: "I would have been outraged if a blind date showed up like that! You showed a lot of restraint!"

Me: "What would you have said?"

Marlene: "Uh, that's a tough one – probably I'd have told him I wasn't hungry."

Me: "You're more disciplined than I am. As I recall, I was hungry. That was a really great restaurant!"

Oops! Hair In The Sink!

This lovely full wall vanity
With His and Hers white sinks
Fulfills my cleaning insanity
While my time-wasting shrinks

My husband's hair is gray
Once brown, I do recall
My reddish strands do stray
I cannot keep them all

I'm careful when I comb
But with our sinks, you see,
A reddish strand might roam
In His sink, cannot be!

Sometimes my own sink's drain
Clogs up and water sits
He claims it's from my mane
That's why the drainage quits

With Draino from the shelf
He fixed it and he vowed
I'd do the next myself
His warning voice was loud

But since his hair is gray
And mine comes from a mix
It's reddish brown today
From "Auburn Number Six"

My problem's all about
My stray hair in His sink
If I don't get it out
He'll have a fit, I think

A new chore on my list
Is hair search every morning
If one red strand is missed
I'll get that Drano warning!

Creativity And The Sexes

Are women more creative than men?
I've pondered this again and again
Well, the Muses were chicks
And the Beach Boys were hicks
But who cares, this is Now, that was Then

Guys had steam rooms while women gave birth
There were mostly male scribes here on earth
While the men drank all night,
Keeping women out of sight,
Male poets had a lock on all mirth;

But that's only history, it seems
If you really believe in your dreams
With no Y chromosome,
Can you still drive it home?
With desire you can now produce reams!

Or if stand-up comedy is your bent
Don't get upstaged and don't be content
If a guy would outdo you,
Just flatly go, "Screw You!"
You can easily outclass the gent.

Why waste time on a sexual war?
Just create while he's deep in a snore
You simply wake earlier
While you make your hair curlier
As he's shaving you even the score;

The big failing which all men have got
Is their arrogance, and they have a lot
While they're gloating all day
You're creating away
And come up with material that's hot!

Most men disdain baths, they take showers
But women bathe creatively for hours
While my man's getting dressed
I'm there fashioning my best
Bathing sharpens my literary powers!

So while hubby sits at his computer
Or perhaps he's a fast-track commuter
It doesn't matter which,
You amazing hot bitch,
Your work's finished and without any tutor!

See, the stuff in your multi-tasked head
Worked itself out while you were in bed
You remembered it all
So when editors call,
You've got gems which they've never quite read!

Sharing An Office

Marlene: "I'm keeping my mouth shut about this whole series."

Me: "You should. It gets worse."

* * *

I share an office with hubby, the wise
Forget those planets, we share different skies
Our tempers flare with rifts I despise
When my outputs fizzle he yells at my cries

This office at home, it ain't up to snuff
For space for operations, there's never enough
I think I'm entitled, he thinks he's tough
He regards my projects as feminist fluff

But because of our budget we have these rules
We weren't born yesterday, we're nobody's fools
If the line is crossed we behave like ghouls
He can't touch my letters, I can't touch his tools;

For any couple who thinks they can share
I have this message: He'll get in your hair
She'll talk when she shouldn't — he gives her the air
For He needs to concentrate — doesn't she care?

But we go on with this, day after day
Even though patience is fading away
We two have to work and we both like to play
So we call a truce while our hairs turn grey

He draws up a strange Mason-Dixon type line
If she dares to cross it or utter a whine
He'll savage her ego, and I need mine
It's not like a job you can easily resign

But I have my leverage, now hear this:
If he wants some lovin', or even one kiss
I know how to throw out one gigantic 'dis'
And I'll confiscate something which he might miss;

If one of us errs, there's consequences galore
I might get squashed if I say any more!
Those countries and sects who are always at war
Might copy from us, we're truced to the core

The Husband Who Kept His Wife Heckled

My husband's not tactful, like the typical man
He chides me and nags me whenever he can
He won't take me seriously when I complain
He's not empathetic if I have a pain

"Oh Honey, I'm worn out! — why can't you be nice?"
"Why don't you lie down?" He's adept at advice
"The vent overhead, dear, is blowing cold air!
"It's right on my head and you don't seem to care!"

"Poor Baby, you're cold — you need a warm coat
"And a glove for your nose and hot tea for your throat."
"The temperature, honey, is too low for me!"
"Use that new wooly throw while you're sipping
   your tea."

"I know you feel warmer and more normal, dear
"You don't seem to understand stuff women fear."
"I do understand it — you're female and weak
"You can't open jar lids with your delicate physique."

"You won't let me choose what we see on TV!"
"Those chick flicks are dumb and don't interest me!"
"When I need a hug, you're too focused to do it!"
"When I'm concentrating, you tell me to screw it!"

"Whenever I get my hair trimmed and restyled
"You don't seem to notice!" "I do too, poor child."
"You don't give me credit for organizing stuff!"
"I married you, sweetheart, and ain't that enough?"

The Man Who Swore At His Computer

Marlene: "Writers are human — humans complain. Sometimes complaining helps a person to make a point."

Me: "Why can't my husband be patient with me? He characterizes all my efforts to have a discussion as some kind of argument."

Marlene: "Many men do that."

Me: "I think I'll write an essay distinguishing a discussion from an argument."

Marlene: "Not now."

* * *

I know a man who started out well
He led a clean life, I'm happy to tell
But then one day he bought a PC
And now he's as ratty as ratty can be

His day is now ruled by the points and the clicks
If things don't go well, **I** could be in a fix
He not only swears at the monitor's nose
He abuses anyone who approaches too close

My marriage has changed since high tech came to town
I once had control over feeling quite down
But now that my man is computer engrossed
I tiptoe around him so I won't be toast

I asked him if he behaved poorly with strangers
I wondered if others avoided these dangers
"No, only when **you** ask me how things are going!"
(He sure let me know my sensitivity is showing.)

From now on whenever he boots up that thing
With me not knowing what the session might bring
I think I will quietly exit the house
And let him enjoy companionship with the mouse.

Youthful Memories And Maternal Concerns

The Boy In The Blue Suit

His first name was Conrad
I don't know his last
Our whirlwind romance
Dates way back in my past

So bright were his eyes
As they looked right at mine
My innocence wondering
If this was a sign

Of feelings so new
Like the first heat of Spring
I must have been blushing
Not saying a thing

He wore a blue suit
With shorts and a vest
And a clean white shirt
That's how he was dressed

Each morning we met
At the same exact place
Not talking, just gazing
At each other's face

We lay on our sides
For it was the rule
On mats we had brought
To take naps in school

I still have his picture
The last day we played
No more kindergarten
But onto first grade

My Progeny

Marlene: "I have more problems with my children than with my grandchildren."

Me: "I've kept my feelings private because I have no control over—"

Marlene: "Don't say it."

Me: "I'll put it in a short poem."

Marlene: "You should make many of your poems shorter!"

Me: "Too late now. I've been influenced too heavily by poets like Keats. All those words about an urn with a message about unravished women. At least he was good at rhymes!"

Marlene: "Many poetry aficionados have abandoned the rhyming poem."

Me: "I have two things to say about that, and it includes poets AND prose writers: One: Most of those authors who write emotionally, like, stream of consciousness types, have a hard time connecting with simple folks. Authors who write with so much description and force you to keep going back to reread what they wrote earlier, are even worse. Take James Joyce, famous for his book 'Ulysses.' My husband thought he was a great writer with a great story. But he had to buy a second book to explain what Ulysses was all about. I have a hard time enjoying some of the deeply emotional non-rhyming poems I've heard lately. Especially if it's a long-winded sermon. I dislike feeling nagged just listening to some-body's verbal assault on the dangers of being human."

Marlene: "Sorry to interrupt before you got to your second point, but if I understand you correctly, you think of yourself as one of those, uh, simple folks?"

Me: "Okay, so I tried to read Ulysses and then the explainer book and lost my patience."

Marlene: "What's your second point?"

Me: "I had a second point?" Oh, of course. Some rhyming poems are so memorable they will live for-ever. Would you really want to read again and again something like, 'I think that I shall never see – a poem as lovely as a gingko plant or a coconut palm . . .'"

Marlene: "Fashions change. Women don't wear hats with feathers any longer."

Me: "You're right. But we got off the subject of short poems versus long ones."

Marlene: "Zzzzzzzzz. ...."

Me: "Marlene???"

* * *

My friends all have grandchildren
I admit I have none
They show me those photographs
Take them out one by one
Or their cellphone is packed
Or their scrapbook's filled pages
I've even seen spreadsheets
Of their progeny by ages

But what can I do
When my kids didn't do it
Their lives took on turns
They didn't get to it
The truth is I love them
They were my dependents
Can I feel remorse
If they don't have descendants?

Careful, Son

I had a young son I named Howard
In school, he was never a coward
His girlfriends were many
He loved one called Penny
Thank God she was never deflowered

Go With The Flow

I wonder if I'll ever see
A babe who didn't pee on me
When I pick up a little guy
I pray that he would please stay dry

But children need to let it go
Soon kiddies learn to train the flow
At last we learn good habits, friends
Until we need to buy Depends.

Falling Through The Generation Gap

Oh My My My!
I realize at last
That my present ideas
Are all in the Past

The more that I think
I know what to claim
The next generation
Is revising the game

The kids that I see
Who have many more votes
Think much younger than me
And they laugh at my quotes

If I say, "That's Swell!"
They look at me funny
They think I'm a nutcase
For saving my money

But I'm just an old-timer
An antique on the nook
I'm classed as a throwback
Like a history book

I don't text while working
I don't drink Red Bull
I still frown on shirking
My nights are not full

I think like a geezer
I dress like a nerd
I'm always a pleaser
My path undeterred

The Aging Author's Lament

Confidence Level

Someone tells me she liked what I wrote
I don't give myself any freedom to gloat
But on my notepad I scribble a note:
"Tell yourself you coined a good quote!"

Electronic Rejection

I asked myself today, what makes me feel better?
A Rejection E-mail or a Rejection Letter?
It matters not that it's "No" or just hinted
My finished book's still not getting printed

My inner ego proclaims I'm still fine
So I roll out the agent list and pour me some wine
But really, I'm still the best unpublished writer
That I ever met, and I'm still a great fighter

So I'll follow the rules that the literates advise
Just keep sending stuff until somebody buys
Even Thomas Edison got his new light bulb shunned
He just kept on plugging while his creditors dunned

Was Thomas just lucky, or bravely persistent?
He worked when computers weren't even existent
When I visit New York, his lights are still there
So I breathe in and out while I'm pulling my hair

I'm glad there is e-mail and I don't have to wonder
Which rubbish in which waste can my manuscript
is under
The authors of bygone days didn't have "Word"
Some wrote by the fire, or so I have heard

So I won't complain — no not ever again
A woman can thrive in a world of strong men
If it's true that the pen is mightier than the sword
Just think of the power my hard drive has stored!

Inspiration And Perspiration

Inspiration is bright and quite breezy
You read a great book sitting down
Perspiration is not quite that easy
Most diligence starts with a frown

The contest you enter is scary
Your goal's not to show, but to win
Contestants have no room to tarry
The needed toil makes your head spin
"Oh why did I seek this position???"
"I could have relaxed and had fun!"
You chafe at endeavor's transition
Your brain freezes 'til you're undone

But nothing in life that's worth living
Is handed to you from the start
It's not what you take -- it's the giving
The prize is expanding your heart.

How To Write Poetry

If your mood is light
Write something bright
If your mood is gloomy
Spill your guts to me

If your mood is mean
Describe the whole scene
Have you got the idea?
Look for your panacea

There are rules to follow
Don't make your words hollow
Try with all your might
Not to pen something trite

Though your blood pressure quickens
Don't borrow from Dickens
If you must scribble rhymes
Skip "the best of times."

You're unique, you know
To be first where you go
Just get inside your mind
For the treasures you'll find

If a small vocabulary
Or a poor dictionary
Leaves your descriptions cold
Set your motor on bold

If anger runs through you
Let a therapist clue you
But if you have to pray it
It's all how you say it!

Amnesia Or Brain Clog?

Marlene: "This is my most scary subject."

Me: "Really?"

Marlene: "Yes, sometimes I forget what I'm doing, like why I went into the room I'm in."

Me: "I have just the poem for you! I think I wrote it ten years ago."

Marlene: "Don't you put dates on your stuff?"

Me: "Yes. But I forget where my stuff is."

* * *

As my eightieth year is encroaching
I feel Father Time's clues fast approaching
When ideas here and there
Vanish into thin air
I believe it is time for some coaching!

Upstairs there are books in my study
To resort to when memory gets muddy
So I head myself there
Pausing right on the stair
Feeling blank like an old fuddy duddy

If a library book was concerned
Was it here, or already returned?
Since I couldn't remember
July from September
It was good to write notes, I had learned

The library was somewhere in town
Instead of upstairs I went down
There I glanced at my note
Saying "Don't Bring a Coat"
"It's July," I recalled, with a frown

So I drove into town with some speed
For that library book I did need
As I got to the place
A strange look took my face
What was it I wanted to read?

But I bravely went on and did enter
That marvelous library center
To the head clerk I said,
"There's a book I once read,
Written by a fine author and mentor."

The clerk asked me the name of the book
"Well, I don't know!" (She gave me a look)
"On Amnesia, I think,
But my memory does stink
The book's here, but I'm not sure which nook!"

The good lady did not even flinch
Being trained to help out in a pinch
"Ma'am, you go to Shelf C
In Section 3D
But my dear, you must search every inch!"

I discovered, alas and alack,
That no book brings my memory back
It's not just a rumor
That old folks need some humor
When we get a 'where am I?' attack!

Losing My Clothes

I know I'm forgetful, but it's getting worse
I can't seem to manage the things in my purse
When I leave the house I go through a list
To not be embarrassed at something I missed;

Like if it might rain with dark clouds in the sky
It helps to have rain gear to keep my hair dry
The day may be hot, but weather is iffy
A mean wind might blow where I freeze in a jiffy

Today it was wet so I wore my raincoat
My memory's bad, so I wrote me a note
Do not leave that coat where it might go astray
With the note in my handbag I soon drove away

The drizzle was constant and nasty and chilly
I got to a meeting and did something silly
I took off the raincoat and sat myself on it
All during the meeting my butt was upon it

But when it was time to adjourn I was talking
To people I knew and then soon I was walking
Right out of the meeting hall out to my car
I had parked very near, so I didn't walk far

I noticed the weather had gotten much better
I got into my car wearing slacks and a sweater
How nice that the rain clouds had drifted away
Leaving puddles that wouldn't be there the next day

When I got to my house, I groped for my coat
But it wasn't there with me in spite of my note
I had to drive all the way back to the place
But when I went to get it, there wasn't a trace

I beseeched the guard "Please help me to find
The coat that I brought that I just left behind
We looked and we looked, but it had disappeared
I loved that nice coat, how I lost it was weird

Then I did remember some other mishaps
Where I lost some gloves, some umbrellas and wraps
I once dropped a hat in the Atlantic Ocean
Once the wind took my scarf and I made a commotion

Then I could add other things gone with the wind
How careless I've gotten — how greatly I've sinned
Some hankies, a shawl, and a bathing suit topper
About three pairs of socks and a pin made of copper

I've probably lost a whole wardrobe I fear
And once clothes are gone they just don't reappear
Especially socks when they're not in the dryer
They were in the wash, but they just took a flyer

At least I can say with conviction and pride
That I never lost pearls which I wore as a bride
I still have a skirt I can barely zip up
And I still have a bra with a double A cup

How Could I Forget You?

It's so good to see you again!
It's been a long time, dear
Your name is stuck in my brain
The part right next to this ear

How's the family, honey?
It's really quite a shame
But isn't it sort of funny,
That I can't remember your name?

I think it starts with an S
No, now I think it's a C
The letters are clicking in, yes!
Don't laugh, t'aint funny, McGee

Ok, now I know — you're Carmen
How could I ever forget
You've always been so charmin'
I'll get your last name yet!

The sound is very pretty
It starts with the letter P
It doesn't ? Oh my, what a pity
You'd better repeat it for me.

Travel And Its After Effects

Commuter Airline Sandwich

I'm crunched between a hunk and a very chic face
Reporting to you from Runway D in my space
Doing that fab non-stop Flight 32
I'm in 19E and now coming to you

My carryon should have been checked, she said
What? Give them my stuff? I'd rather be dead
While waiting for earphones I'm reading guys' lips
I believe they're giving out traveling tips

Oh Orville, did you ever think your invention
Would sandwich vast numbers? Was that your
intention?
A sandwich should act like a corned beef on rye
Not crammed in Seat E and surely not I

The earphones won't muffle that wee puppy's yelping
From inside his cage whose confines aren't helping
Some flights have loud coughers, some small infants crying
Some people ask questions who shouldn't be flying

Oh, there I go judging, I can't seem to stop
I'll probably be complaining 'til the sun blows its top
Miss? Pass me those nuts while reciting the weather
We commuter line sandwiches must stick close together!

At The Grand Canyon In The Big Leather Chair

Resting is what I lately do best
Trail walking puts me to quite a test
Watching for rocks while seeing the West
A rock that fits my rear end's truly blessed

Sitting inside on that big antique chair
Wondering who else once sat right there
A beautiful girl with long golden hair?
Or a rejected lad trying hard not to care

Folks walk by me and one nods his head
He sees I'm resting (not better off dead)
I'm coddling my body after eating that bread
Digestion is tiresome, someone once said

When I go back East where the trails are easier
And walking up lower hills slightly less breezier
Eating a breakfast that's definitely cheesier
Makes me realize I'm getting much geezier

Footnotes

When I'm going away on a trip with my hubby
That's when I wish I weren't so chubby
But God designed me the way that I am
Why didn't he make me hate bagels with jam?

I have arthritis in both of my feet
Which means I shuffle to the place where we eat
It's not so awful to walk quite slow
As long as I get where we're needing to go

When a woman is short -- I'm 4 feet eleven
It means I'll be noticed in the choir in heaven
They always put all the shorties in front
With arthritis eliminated! That's what I want!

So while I'm not going to win any races
I've got many pictures of wonderful places
I walked my whole heart out in Cuzco Peru
And again in Cambodia, for I went there too

But while on an Angkor Wat tour of the site
My feet followed tourists who turned to the right
But my tour pals went left soon looking around
For that slow-walking lady who couldn't be found

An hour without me and they called the police
Who didn't speak English — just Cambodianese
Then one lad was able to get me a lift
On one fellow's motorcycle — boy, was he swift!

And the best part about that whole frightening test?
I viewed that whole site while my feet got to rest!
There's always a bright spot in every dark day
As long as one thinks in a positive way

If some body parts need some medical attention
There's some genius out there with some new invention
Whether pills or new braces that help us a lot
We oldies should thank every gift we just got!

Roughing It At 82

My husband/photographer wants to go on a trip
As his wedded assistant, I must button my lip
Our new destination is a great place out West
Where my camera and wallet hang low on my chest

"We're booked at a motel — no internet there."
"I wonder if I'll get to curl my straight hair."
"They have some electric, but no microwave."
"So I get no warm croissant, but you get to shave?"

"It's just for a week and what shots we can take!"
"I can't hike like you do, so give me a break!"
"The hiking is easy, even with your bad knee."
"I'll sit on that camp chair or lean on a tree."

"You love the Grand Canyon, we've been there before!"
"Right now my blue heating pad's what I adore!"
"Come on, you're a trooper — you can rest on a log."
"But you always get lost — I'm your seeing eye dog!"

"That North Rim is fabulous — fewer visitors honey!"
"Is that why those old cabins rent for big money?"
"The landscapes are the finest in all of the world!"
"I'm sold, dear, who cares if my hair isn't curled!"

So this trip that we're taking to America's wonder
Needs planning --which stack is my to-do list under?
That North Rim's high altitude so far from a town
Means respecting the edge — it's a lot further down

But I'm only 82 and still young at heart
I've traveled a lot and at prepping I'm smart
In one suitcase clothes and cosmetics must fit
But I need a good cane and my blood pressure kit

With all of these worries I still sleep at night
At my age it's not likely that I'll die of fright
My need for adventure is still pretty strong
But the list for my packing is three pages long!

Is My Clothes Closet Too Small?
(Or do I keep too much stuff???)

I keep wrapping paper supplies
(For those birthday gifts surprise)
In a corner under my dresses
Do I wear them? No more guesses!

There are garment bags and boxes
Finding jackets? one outfoxes
There's a shredder on a shelf
Can I reach it by myself?

I need someone to assist me
Ah, that husband who just kissed me!
"Honey, help me reach my sweaters!
But please don't tip that box of letters!"

"Why so many pairs of shoes?
How much weight did you not lose?
I see eighteen different sizes!"
(I've got problems, he surmises)

There are suitcases well travelled
And a wool scarf that unraveled
I see gloves that felt fantastic
And some lunch kits made of plastic

I won't now describe the rest
It's a storage horror at best
For a woman with my stuff
One clothes closet's not enough!

Would a house with more square feet
Let me keep my clothes more neat?
Or should I decide one day
To give half my things away?

Then I'd have to make decisions
Make some effort for revisions
I'm a helpful loving wife,
But my closet holds my life!!!

Modern Art

Picasso

I love Picasso's paintings
How he lets his brush roam free
He really dug shapely women
Painting boobs where butts should be.

Was Jackson Pollock
A Real Artist?

I went to the Metropolitan Museum of Art
Saw the gallery I wanted to see
"The real modern stuff," I told the guard
"That's for me!"

My eyesight was pretty good that day
My corrective eyeglasses didn't get in the way
But when I saw that unbelievably large canvas
Labeled "Jackson Pollock," with that usual descriptive tag,
It said "Autumn Rhythm, Number 30, 1950"

Well, I was new to this medium, or should I say style
Although I'd quickly realized, unfortunately,
Only rich people could buy a painting with His name
I asked the wall, because the guard was standing tall
"What is this painting about?"
He had an expression on his face the notion I
shouldn't ask

But luck was with me! There was a bench right there!
I could sit and ponder those so-called brush strokes
"He must have been very nervous," I thought,
"This Pollock fellow,
"Because in order to contain all this focused fury,
"Avoiding colors like green, blue, orange and yellow,
"He learned discipline in art school, I guess!"

As I continued to stare at the black swirls and dots
Also the beige background, was that the canvas unpainted?
Whew how long did it take the guy?
And why am I getting nervous just gazing at it?
I know! It's hypnotic!

I'm being swept up into the maelstrom like a dizzy dance!
I'd better see if the guard notices! Okay, I get it!
It's my unconscious talking! Absolutely!
That's why I came here! To avoid my own darkness!
It's taking me back to my childhood I believe....

As a little girl of four I would chalk up a sidewalk
Sometimes I'd put in circles and even a few words
My mother found me and said: "Come away now, child,
"You're getting your slacks dirty!"
So I must have decided then I shouldn't be an artist.
Is that why I became a struggling writer???

Marlene: "You told me you weren't into poetry that didn't rhyme! And now this!!!"

Me: "I know, but as I decided to write about abstract art, my brain seemed to go that way."

Marlene: "Is it catching? You know I always write in nearly perfect meter!"

Me: "I'm a poet – not a psychologist! There has to be a reason why I loved that painting."

Marlene: "Sounds like it was too big to fit on a wall unless you owned a mansion."

Me: "So I bought the Pollock book at the Met. If I can't afford the artwork, I —"

Marlene: "The bookstores at museums try to display books that they exhibit — I know this because —"

Me: "I also bought a scarf with an abstract design. It's so soft and —"

Marlene: "You interrupted me. I was trying to help you with your budget!"

Me: "It's too late for that. But I decided to buy the book because —"

Marlene: "I know why — so you could —"

Me: Why can't either of us complete our sentences?"

Marlene: "I'll keep quiet if you like."

Me: "No, just let's face it. When the drip painting took off and became a hot property, artists and non-artists alike got enthusiastic. Maybe it influenced poets too."

Marlene: "Mmmm."

Me: Oh, come on! I didn't mean to shut you up!!"

* * *

Scary Movie About A Painting

You readers out there
I'm sure you can guess
Which old movie story
Is it? Well, I confess

It's that Dorian Gray guy
The 22-year-old male
Whose entire life wish was:
Only bread could get stale

He had to stay young
But what of his soul?
He could ruin women
Eternal youth was his goal

He commissioned a painting
While handsome as ever
He stayed that way always
And the painting? Hah! Never

A fellow named Albright
Did the horrible face
I shrieked in that theatre
"Get me outta this place!!!"

Marlene: "I see you're back to rhyming and I—"

Seeing Isn't Believing

I know that this artist had something to prove
So he put a slash in the canvas
Did I get the message right?
Was he feeling good that day?
I don't know what else to say

I read about emerging American women artists
They were very bold in their creations
Men ruled but they weren't brave ladies
Mary Cassatt painted mothers with babies

Louise Nevelson never got over building blocks
Neither did I, but I was fearful of structures much
taller than me
So I did little things
Like paint a very small tree

I went to the Dali Museum in Saint Pete
Took my son there for a new visual treat
He liked the idea of clocks melting, saying: "That's
the Greatest!!"
Maybe it was his nature. Of my three kids, he talked
the latest.

The Art Of Abstract Art

I like abstract art just because it's abstract
I don't have to buy it, and that's just a fact
My simplified method to shine and impress
Is to visit museums where you gaze at success

The art museum's great and it doesn't cost much
An Art Expo's good, if you look and don't touch
A middle-class woman might pine for Van Gogh
But to bring the art home you must first have the
dough

I once had a goal that I'd be a collector
I'd go to garage sales and become a detector
But after my many pursuits of the FIND
My numerous buys were not one of a kind

I read lots of art books and own quite a few
I'm well versed in Pollock and Rauschenberg too
But art is my hobby — can't draw a straight line
So I married an artist, and that worked out fine!!!

Quarantining Isn't Normal – Fretting Is

When You Turn Away From Trouble

Wash your hands with sanitizer
Elbow bump — it's so much wiser
Save your money — be a miser
Look for cures from Roche or Pfizer!

Guard your mate if his eyes wander
Honor the doctor and first responder
Shop for hair dye to be blonder
Think of life and quietly ponder

Try new recipes — buy a new jam
Invent new ways to spruce up ham
Read all warnings — time to cram
Be a virus avoider! Guess I now am!

If You Feel Like A Teen, Can You Still Quarantine?

I once had that bad Scarlet Fever
The "Stay Out!" door sign was bright red
Everyone knew I was ailing
I was truly confined to my bed

I re-read all of my comic books
Elmer Fudd was my usual hero
That hated thermometer's silver
Kept landing too far above zero!

So now that I'm eighty years plus
It's stay home time so I've been told
Can't do parties or movies or shop
Having lunch with the girls is too bold

"Aha!" is what I tell callers
This confinement is not a big deal
I once was fourteen with that fever
So now I know just how to feel!

I still have my Mickey Mouse funnies
And Young Adult books on my shelf
I've learned that it's best to stay healthy
I've always loved coddling myself!

A Poem About Confinement

I'm looking at my bedroom wall
It needs to be painted a different shade of white
What happened to my life?
I'll be in a better mood tonight.

The Itty-Bitty Virus

The itty-bitty virus
Got into someone's mouth
That person coughed and
Soon the world went South!

Soon all the humans
Had to stay in place
While the itty-bitty virus
Still wanders toward one's face.

What Will I Accomplish?

What will I accomplish
This day that's so fair
The sky is bright blue
With the virus out there

I could write a sonnet
About how I feel
With good wishes on it
But bad vibes are real

I'm on this great planet
But so is this virus
My friends are all wailing
Nobody will hire us!

So who do we blame?
Put the "perps" in one lump?
Or governments all
On whom shall we dump?

We're just being tested
By the powers that be
Please, unseen marauder,
Just let me be me!

Marlene: "That poem is making me scratch. Reminds me of some spider rhyme."

Me: "If I'm going to borrow from somebody else's written stuff, I just do it! It's not a crime to dive into our literary depositary of songs kids still sing."

Marlene: "Well, I'm still feeling nervous about it."

Me: "There's a pill for that. Try re-reading my poem: 'Pills and More Pills.' "

Marlene: "You're supposed to be a poet — not a doctor."

Me: " I am a doctor. I have a J.D. degree."

Marlene: "Oh, your lawyer credential. That's even worse!"

Optimism For The Pessimists

Still Flipping Hamburgers
(For All These Years)

We buy ground meat for our four-burner stove
Our dry food pantry holds a large treasure trove
I search for the garlic salt — where did it go?
Oh, still on the counter — that's so good to know

The truth about frying lean ground meat is this:
When you flip a patty, sometimes you might miss
Failure's no option when it's time for dinner
The cook's job's forever, and I'm no beginner!

But here's the good news – I'm still out there flipping
I still have my job, although there's no tipping
There's grease on the stove when I'm done with the frying
I clean up my mess 'cause there's no use in crying!

Marlene: "Oh, now we're back to the fat again? I thought you reformed about that!"

Me: "You're my conscience, so you get to rib me and render me, but not scorch me!"

Marlene: "Let me review our agreement again. Didn't I have oversight over your behavior?"

Me: "I guess so. So what should I do if my spouse loves hamburgers?"

Marlene: "Well, you can cook them, but you don't have to eat them."

Me: "You mean, inhale all those aromas and then just chew on a snack bar with raisins, nuts, caramel, whole grain oats, sugar, canola oil, rice flour, brown sugar, syrup, salt, baking soda, --"

Marlene: "Well, that's what modern enlightened women have to do to stay photogenic!"

Me: "I, I can't, I, uh, oh, well, I have one thing to say!"

Marlene: "What's that?"

Me: "My husband knows how to take photos of me and then do touch up to enhance my looks."

Marlene: "Sounds complicated. How much work does he have to do to make you look, uh, less, oh, you know, more youthful?

Me: "Well, the photo file is between one and two gigabytes."

Marlene: "I think I made my point."

Me: "You didn't even ask about pixels or layers!!! That's another — uh, what are you snacking on now?"

Wedding Photos

My first husband didn't smile in our professionally
ordered wedding photos
I guess he could foretell the future.

My second husband did smile when our wedding
picture was taken.
Actually, he always smiled
Even when he was sleeping.

My third husband was much better at predictions
He let his brother take our photo as we cut the cake
This spouse of mine eventually became an art
photographer
Wow! Did we ever catch a break!!!

Was I Too Pessimistic?

Instead of the pleasure just offered
The fog of old dreams pass on by
How many wishes were never fulfilled?
Invitations without a reply?

When a compliment from someone grateful
Seemed painfully hard to take in
Plus accomplishments promptly forgotten
Why didn't I feast on a win?

In four decades reviewing this lifetime
I should cancel all times of regret
When grasping the warmth of my pillow
Let me savor those joys that come yet.

Is My Attitude Being Tested In My Dreams?

In reviewing my dreams there's an attitude riddle
My dozing should not feed such worry
Is my unconscious where I rage or belittle?
And makes me wake up in a hurry?

As I sleep I see bad news and problems arising
And feel there's no peace in the land
There are people harassing me — it's so surprising
Sweet me? I just don't understand!

Maybe it's good that I'm not good at frowning
In photos I don't pout — I smile
When folks start to argue, I'm joking and clowning
Happiness words suit my style

I have to believe I'm a human with feeling
And submerging the grief for joy's sake
I'd rather enjoy life — is that not revealing?
More hours with fun while awake!!!

Feeling Good About Feeling Bad

This story's about Optimism, you see
But that word isn't all that it's cracked up to be
"The glass is half full", you say under your breath
"I'm going to be cheerful, though feeling like death!"

Now everyone knows bad news gets in the way
There's something to moan about every damned day
The insurance didn't cover your medical bill?
Relax, and enjoy it, it's a new kind of thrill

Your stomach is hurting over something you ate?
Pretend you're a thoroughbred poised at the gate
Some trainers put blinders on thoroughbreds' eyes
Put blinders on yours and tell yourself lies:

Your retirement nest egg is getting much fatter
Your dream of financial success didn't shatter!
Your kid didn't call you about her divorce?
Remember your strength and remember that horse

That eyeglass prescription isn't really much stronger
Your walk to the store didn't really take longer
That fine travel agent didn't cancel your cruise
And your day at the racetrack? You did not really lose

Your shoulders don't hunch and you seem a bit taller
Those spots on your arms are all getting much smaller
Your jokes get big laughs and your calls get returned
You take many chances but never get burned

I could go on and on, but I'm too busy smiling
I can't wait to tackle my backlog of filing
My memory's great and my limbs never ache
I never need spell-check and hate birthday cake

I never procrastinate and never miss calls
I never get spots on my rugs or my walls
My thighs are as smooth as when I was a girl
I have no trouble getting my lashes to curl

It's eternally sunny when I go to the beach
I'm less than five feet, but I have a long reach
I really believe all this bullshit I tell you
If you also believe it, there's a bridge I can sell you

The one thing that's true about optimism, friend
Is, it's good to feel happy and smile to the end!

Marlene: "Can I go home now?"

Acknowledgments

THE PUBLISHING OF A POETRY COLLECTION requires an assortment of facilitators whose assistance makes such a book possible. Many of the poems included in this book were written years ago, although a significant batch of them were written or rewritten during the last two years. When Penelope Love, my publication consultant throughout this project, suggested I write some verse pertinent to the widening global Covid-19 pandemic, I needed to adapt my humorous and often lackadaisical style to the seriousness of what was happening to readers and poetry lovers all over the world. The result of her suggestion became those five poems included in the category "Quarantining Isn't Normal – Fretting Is!" The bulk of the material in this sixth published book of mine was edited and refined by me after March of 2020, the month that most of the United States began to suffer from the confinement measures instituted by governmental authorities requiring the altered habits of all of us who have been affected. Instead of attending my weekly writers' group critique sessions and my monthly Ballenisles Book Club meetings, I began my new lifestyle, which included learning how to attend a "Zoom Meeting" and avoiding many of my former recreational outings.

Writing poetry for me does not involve the type of research or technical help that a typical book, whether non-fiction or fiction, requires. The poet needs moral support, life experience, writing tools, communication tools, plus the ordinary products that keep a woman of my age as healthy as possible. My acknowledgments are the following:

For assisting me with cover design, biographical content, brevity instead of wordiness where appropriate, and other parts that make up a book such as *Think Yourself Young*, I acknowledge the sturdy and conscientious efforts of Marlene Klotz, a fellow author. As for making it possible for me to digest a much wider scope of published literary material, I acknowledge my friends, Barry Weiss, Barbara Hurwit, Pat Williams,

Mimi Paris, Ellen Weisberg, Carol White, Anne Farley Gaines and the late Elizabeth Pomada. In the case of Mrs. Pomada, whose books about America's Painted Ladies first lured me to attend her San Francisco Writers Workshop and encouraged me to continue to work on my humorous prose after I attended and worked with her at two of those conferences at the InterContinental Mark Hopkins hotel on Nob Hill, I have not forgotten the elements of her guidance.

In a departure from what I perceive as the traditional way a writer thanks those persons who have helped in the publication of a book, I'd like to acknowledge those tireless and brave workers who have gone to work during the ravages of the virus despite the risk to their safety: all the employees of the Target Store on Okeechobee Road in Royal Palm Beach where I buy my food and other goods, the cashiers and employees of the Publix store on Okeechobee Road in the "Shoppes at Andros Isle" shopping center, where I also buy my food, and the employees of the Office Depot store at Southern Boulevard and State Route 7 in Wellington, where I buy my office supplies and receive technical computer assistance, which I need so desperately at times. These people whose faces have been partially covered with masks have made this book possible. No author can work without food, clothing, medical supplies or technical assistance in today's world.

I also acknowledge my various doctors and their assisting professionals in keeping me as fit as a lady of my vintage can manage. There are too many people whose names are not included here—too many medical workers and too many back room working people who travel to their workplaces every day that I have either met occasionally or those whom I have never met, but who deserve to be acknowledged because I'm still able to put words on a desktop computer and then send those words to a publisher.

God Bless them all.

Sincerely,

Lea Hope Becker

A Poem In Memory Of Dorothy

You came to me with flowers
Did I notice that your skin was darker than mine?
Maybe, but our differing shades were overshadowed
By our new next-door neighbors' kinship

As women married to men and with grown children
We shared our stories
You were from the South and I from the North
Our kids and our husbands also
But the similarities outweighed the differences

You wanted to lose weight and exercise it off!
I wanted to lose weight and do it by magic
Only after you had conquered the pounds
Did your illness do further work
I greeted you at the rehab center with a photo

The photo was of a flower that you could barely see
Lying in bed while I pretended I was your nurse
Soon you'd be home again, I prayed,
But when you finally arrived you were leaving
Headed toward a better and more peaceful place

I cried when your daughter told me the truth
Bent over I tried to remember the faith you taught me
We were all related, you know
Maybe when you arrived, I'd follow you there
What flowers would I bring?

The funeral was attended by myriads of folks
Their shades mostly all darker than mine
Yet we all stood in mourning, then praising
I will keep your beautiful memory book
Forever in my heart.

Goodbye to walking with you on this ground, Dorothy
Hello to hearing the cries of those still here
Wishing that we could all walk together in friendship
Are you watching us now, hoping we will succeed?
Women, men, and children, all caring in our hearts.

About The Author

LEA HOPE BECKER began writing poems and short stories when she was a ten-year-old growing up in a crowded Chicago, Illinois neighborhood. As a youngster, she possessed a vivid imagination and adored writing, and her interest in literary pursuits never waned. As time progressed, Lea decided upon a career that ultimately led to becoming a tax attorney. But beneath the spreadsheets, her desire to become a published author smoldered.

At age seventy, after years spent in her lawyer profession, she wrote and published her first book, a humorous memoir of her childhood, which included her own illustrations. In quick succession four more humor books were published, two memoirs and two fictional stories "laced with humor." In her own words:

My writing reflects how I feel about life, including my belief that laughter is still the best way to achieve well-being. I enjoy writing stories to make people happy, not sad or angry.

As so many of her devoted followers have said, "A book written by Lea can brighten the darkest day."

She lives with her illustrator/photographer husband and writes books in West Palm Beach, Florida. After having her home and workplace in heavily populated suburban Chicago for many years, she remarried and relocated to rural Upstate New York. Lea and her husband began longing for less challenging winters a decade later and moved to enjoy the warmth of South Florida, where they currently work at home and find time to travel for pleasure. Her poem "I Love South Florida Weather," is a reversal of the way "snowbirds" think. By simply reading this poem, the reader can visualize Lea decked out on a beach chair ready to take in the sunshine during an overheated summer day, when a sudden tropical storm arrives, leaving her alone, shivering from the wind, and running for cover, but still laughing at how quickly a planned schedule can become unraveled. If you asked her how she is able to still feel upbeat, she'd most likely reply: "It's become such a good excuse to catch up on those extension tax returns for my nervous clients!"

www.LeaHopeBecker.com

Publisher's Note

Thank you for reading *Think Yourself Young: Laugh Yourself to Life*. Please pass the torch of connection by helping other readers find this book. Here are suggestions for your consideration:

- Write a customer review wherever books are sold.
- Gift this book to friends, family, and colleagues.
- Share a photo of yourself with the book on social media and tag #leahopebecker and #thinkyourselfyoung.
- Bring in Lea Hope Becker as a speaker for your club or organization.
- Suggest *Think Yourself Young* to your local book club.
- Recommend *Think Yourself Young* to the manager of your local book store.
- For bulk orders, contact the publisher at 828-585-7030 or email Orders@CitrinePublishing.com.
- Connect with the author at www.LeaHopeBecker.com.

Your book reviews, social media shares and emails are received with heartfelt gratitude.